I0476825

Effective Skills Training
A Guide for Customer Service Skills in the Workplace

Information gathered is exclusively taken from C.D. Johnson experiences over the years from Customer Service Trainings

Cover layout & designed by C.D. Johnson and Diverse Skills Center in Tampa, FL 33687

Printed in the United States of America

ISBN-13: 978-1522870876
ISBN-10: 1522870873

Effective Skills Training

CONTENTS

Introduction

Developing Great Skills with Exceptional Services

If your company prides itself on excellence, then you'll want to invest in this manual.

Exposing this teaching to your company will show your employees how to achieve great customer service skills that will achieve your company over the top!

From 1 to 1,000 employees, this information caters to all...

Having great ideas are awesome, but listening to your customers will affect your company's status, integrity and reputations.

About us:

D.S.C. is owned and operated by Cynthia D. Johnson of CDJ Promos, Inc.

In early 2004, the idea came to Ms. Johnson due to her trials and errors with customer services.

Worked in a GPS corporation where the career change was quite challenging.

Ms. Johnson's background was Medical Electronics where she assisted with a Hematology lab gathering information and performing protocols for reliability Engineer's Departments.

Though her expertise is in Medical Electronics, a downsize of that company, being there for 27 years, forced her to moved back to Central Florida in 2006 to start over again.

With a Customer Service Agency, hiring her to work from home, being a Cyber Agent, worked for an outsourced agent for such companies as: Dinning Reservationists, Office Supplies and Technical Support Departments.

This gave Ms. Johnson the idea to think about what it took to make a customer ecstatic.

Being hired for the GPS Company in 2007, Ms. Johnson had no idea what she was up against.

Not only was it not within her level of choice, but the vertical of this company was hard to comply with.

Through hard work and constant challenges, Ms. Johnson not only exceeded the company's expectations, but was voted Customer Service "Personal of the Year", along with every quarter in 2009.

Asked to head up the training for customer service skills, Ms. Johnson had access to great books and resources such as Dale Carnegie and Carol A. Silvis.

Being willing to share knowledge with application with an awesome attitude, your customers will call and ask for you by name.

What a great asset your name will have inside your company's structure.

CUSTOMER SERVICE DEVELOPMENT SKILLS

"Developing Customer Service Qualities"

"Move Ahead Of Your Competitors"

In Sales Qualities it takes a special person to sell big.

For you to be successful in selling there are several sales qualities you must develop to move ahead of your competitors.

The qualities are:

Loving people - this is important regardless of your background.

If you plan to move to the top you must be willing to love helping people at all levels in your organization.

If you love people you will succeed.

Your attitudes - as much as possible try and have a positive attitude. This will help you whenever you come across some challenges in your buslness.

Your determination/eagerness to succeed - you have made up your mind to be successful, and have set goals to achieve them.

Respect other people's opinion - as well as expecting the same in return.

Patience - this is needed because success does not come overnight.

Other Sales Qualities - **loving your product** - you must love your product, and have a good knowledge about it.

Not only should you love the product, but you should use the product yourself. Be a market of your products or services.

Persistence - this is essential especially when it comes to following up a prospect or customer.

By you following up a prospect it could lead to a sale for your product/service.

Honesty - customers need to know that you are an honest person.

For example, if a prospect tells you not to give out their e-mail address, you not giving it to anyone, shows that you are honest by keeping that promise.

Gaining trust - building a relationship comes first, then listening to what they say.

Why? Because you are showing them that you care, and not just wanting to sell them something. This is when you will gain their trust.

Ask quality questions - this is to determine the prospect's situation and buying needs.

By you asking the prospect questions you are discussing the benefits of your products and services that are mostly related to each customer.

Work hard - you see, most people love the success, but are not prepared to work for it.

Working hard will cause you to talk to more people and will encourage you to be consistently looking for prospects.

Keep in contact with clients - Keeping in contact with clients is showing that they are important to you and your business.

You constantly keeping in touch will keep your name in the customers' mind.

You can send thank you cards or birthday cards when it is their birthday.

CUSTOMER'S COMPLAINTS

How to Encourage Customer Complaints

(a) Open Details

The best way to encourage complaints and comments is to have open contact details. Include a contact address, phone number, and email address on all correspondence, allowing customers to contact you immediately and easily in the event of a problem. The quicker they can contact you, the quicker you can solve their problems.

(b) Friendly Staff

Having friendly and helpful staff will encourage customers to talk about problems they are having with your business, helping to solve problems before they happen. Friendly staff will also help you to deal with complaints, listening to customers rather than trying to argue with them.

(c) Comment Slips

Give customers the opportunity to tell you how they feel about your business. Provide them with comment slips or invite large customers to speak with you personally about how they feel about your business.

On correspondence, state that you are open to contact on problems, e.g. "If you have any problems, do not hesitate to contact us." Etc...

If you invite comment, then people are more likely to respond, giving you a better look at the both the positive and negative areas of your business, and allowing you to deal with them as necessary.

How to Deal with Customer Complaints

It is a fact of business life that not all customers will be happy, even in the finest run businesses, problems, mistakes, or even bad luck can cause people to be dissatisfied with your products or service: hence 'customer complaints'.

When people are unhappy, they will often complain. Many businesses tend to try and ignore complaints, or pass them off as irrelevant, however, if dealt with well, they can actually provide your business with a strong advantage.

The following is a look at some of the ways in which your customers might complain, and how you can deal with them, and turn an unhappy customer into a satisfied one.

Types of Customer Complaints

(a) Letters

Letters are a very common form of complaint; they are generally seen as the most official way of complaining. This means that most customers will only use a letter of complaint where they feel there is a serious dissatisfaction, and where the business has a separate address for complaints or head office.

Letters have an advantage to your business, as they allow you time to look at a problem, solve it, and reply to the customer; hopefully ensuring they are satisfied enough to remain a customer.

(b) Spoken Word to Employees

The most common form of complaint, particularly in retail businesses; is face to face with an employee (usually the front line staff). This could take the form of a passing word or gesture, and can be for small or large problems.

Typical comments include things such as: "This is not the first time…", "I can't believe that…" or even a 'tut' noise in a sentence. They are generally informal complaints or comments, only occasionally do they turn into full scale complaints.

Although there is no official complaint in most cases, spoken word comments can provide information on the everyday problems that customers are experiencing, and provide an opportunity for your employees to solve these problems, both for these customers, and for future ones.

(c) Phone Calls

These are another common form of complaint, generally used for informal minor complaints, but can also be used by a highly dissatisfied customer who does not wish to write. The frequency of phone complaints generally depends on how much your business uses the phone; a call centre will receive many more complaints than a basic office line.

Phone complaints allow you to look into a problem, but do not usually give you as much time to solve it as a letter or email.

(d) Email

Emails are similar to letters; however they tend to describe smaller problems that are expected to be solved in a much quicker time. The number of email complaints you receive will depend mostly on how widely you use email, and whether there is a specific enquiry or complaints email address.

Why You Need to Listen to Customer Complaints

There are many reasons why you should listen to, and respond to your customers complaints; the following are some of the most important:

(a) Development

The most important reason why you should listen to complaints is very simple. If someone is complaining, the chances are, there is a problem in your products or service that is causing it. Listening to complaints allows you to find out what the problems are with your business, and solve them.

Customers satisfied may cost money; you may need to give refunds or replacements, but you will normally regain much more than this over time by retaining the customer.

Fixing a problem once will help you keep the customer who made the complaint, but fixing it permanently will help keep all customers satisfied, and maybe even help to bring in some new customers.

(b) Loyalty

It has been shown in several pieces of research that customers who complain, and have a problem solved are generally much more loyal than those who are simply happy with the business.

If you can fix a complaint quickly, it shows not only that your business respects the customer and wishes to provide a good service; but also that you can be relied upon, even when things go wrong. It can provide a customer with a sense of security in your business, making them much less likely to go to your competitors.

Click here for our article:

(c) Lost Customers

There is a basic choice with dissatisfied customers; Let them complain, and try to solve their problems; or watch them go to your competitors.

Although there are few proven figures, most experts believe that you are up to 10 times more likely to keep a complaining customer (whose problem you try to solve) than you are one who says nothing.

You should also remember that it costs up to five times as much to win a new customer than to keep an old one, even if keeping a dissatisfied customer costs you now, in the long run, it will almost certainly save you money.

If a customer complains, it gives you a chance to make them satisfied with your business again, and for this reason, you should encourage dissatisfied customers to complain.

(d) Employees

If a complaint is the result of a mistake by an employee, a complaint will help you to know where problems lie. Minor problems can be fixed by reminding employees of certain information or processes, major problems can be looked at over a period of time, with the aim of long term improvements. In repeated cases of employee fault, you should consider giving verbal warnings.

Front line employees can often bear the complaints caused by other employee's mistakes, but attempting to solve all problems revealed by complaints will help to keep your customers happy. Matters can also be helped if you give employees enough training and empowerment to deal with complaints and problems quickly, see links section for further information.

"Handling Customer Complaints and Six Steps on How to Solve Them"

Handling Customer Complaints - sometimes from time to time there will be some customer/customers who will be dissatisfied with something you have done in your business.

So, when a problem arise it is best you solve it as soon as possible.

Nine times out of ten when the complaint is dealt with quickly the customer will continue to do business with you and you will gain their trust.

You see, it shows that you were listening to them. Therefore, they will trust you.

It shows that you care about them.

In handling customer complaints - here for you are a few steps on how to solve them.

1. Stay calm - When they are arguing it is best to stay calm because it takes two people to argue.

It also helps because you can never win arguing with a customer.

2. Let the customer vent - you see, some angry customers just need to let off steam.

When you allow them to let off stream without talking back, they will eventually calm down.

It is then and only then can you deal with the problem at hand without being too emotional.

3. Listen - you should try and listen to what the customer has to say. Continue to listen if the complaint cannot be solved immediately.

For example, you send them an audio tape in the mail, but they did not receive it.

To solve the problem you could say something like "I will follow-up or "I will call you back in an hour".

4. Apologize - As soon as you realize who has caused the complaint try to say you are "sorry".

5. Admit - If you realize that you were in the wrong (it was your fault), try and humble yourself in these circumstances. It is best to admit you when you are wrong.

6. Decision - If the customer continues to complain try your best to solve it.

Afterwards, make a decision as to whether or not you need to do business with this customer.

When you have made your decision then move on.

Important Statements You Can Use:

(a) Try and use statements such as "I agree".

(b) "I understand".

(c) "I realize this was inconvenient for you".

Why? It shows that you understand and that you care.

Usually, a dissatisfied customer is not trying to hurt you.

Most of them were hurting long before they've had their dissatisfaction with you.

Handling customer complaints are easy to solve if the cause of the complaint is dealt with professionally and immediately.

Solutions to Customer Complaints:

1. Listen

2. Take Responsibility for your failure to perform

3. Ask the expectations of the customer

4. Listen actively and acknowledge what is being said

5. Recognize the customer's emotions, however, don't react in an emotional way

6. Find out what would make the customer happy

7. Show your concern for the reputation of your company

8. Search for a solution

9. Be willing to take responsibility for the solution

10. Never yield to pressure, only to principle

Steps to Resolving Customer Complaints

1. Listen Intently: Listen to the customer, and do not interrupt them. They need to tell their story and feel that they have been heard.

2. Thank Them: Thank the customer for bringing the problem to your attention. You can't resolve something you aren't completely aware of, or may be making faulty assumptions about.

3. Apologize: Sincerely convey to the customer your apology for the way the situation has made them feel. This is not the time for preachy reasons, justifications or excuses; you must apologize.

4. Seek the Best Solution: Determine what the customer is seeking as a solution. Ask them; often they'll surprise you for asking for less than you initially thought you'd have to give—especially when they perceive your apology and intention is genuinely sincere.

5. Reach Agreement: Seek to agree on the solution that will resolve the situation to their satisfaction. Your best intentions can miss the mark completely if you still fail to deliver what the customer wants.

6. Take Quick Action: Act on the solution with a sense of urgency. Customers will often respond more positively to your focus on helping them immediately versus than on the solution itself.

7. Follow-up: Follow-up to ensure the customer is completely satisfied, especially when you have had to enlist the help of others for the solution delivery. Everything up to this point will be for naught if the customer feels that "out of sight is out of mind."

Problems happen. It's how you honestly acknowledge and handle them which counts with people. Customers will remember you, and happily give you another chance to delight them when you choose to correct problems with the very best you can offer, proving you value them and their business.

SUMMARY:

Do Not Forget!

No matter how bad a problem is, no employee should be subjected to any personal insults or threats from a complaining customer.

Encourage complaints rather than silence, but customers must not be allowed to threaten your employees in any way.

Summary/Key Points

Key points taken from the article...

- Even well run businesses will receive complaints at some point.
- Letters of complaint are generally used for bigger companies, particularly where there is a serious problem.
- Spoken word complaints are common, especially in retail businesses, and can be used for all types of complaint.
- Phone and email complaints are generally used for less serious complaints, but generally need to be dealt with more quickly than letter complaints.
- Complaints allow you to see the faults in your business and fix them.

- Customer who have a problem solved successfully are often more loyal than those who never had a problem in the first place!
- Customers who complain are much (up to 10 times) more likely to stay with your business than those who say nothing.
- Winning a new customer costs up to 5 times more than keeping an old one.
- Complaints can point to weaknesses in your staffing and systems, allowing you to help make improvements.
- Always listen politely to complaint, and offer as much help as possible. Always offer some form of solution, even if it is not exactly what the customer asked for.
- Keep your details open, allowing customers to contact you quickly and easily, consider offering comment slips to keep up to date with how they feel your business is running.
- No matter how badly a customer has been treated, never allow your employees to feel threatened by them.

Contact

To set up consultation with Diverse Skills Center's for any additional information regarding effective skills training for personal or business, you may reach the company at:

Diverse Skills Center

P.O. Box 290963

Tampa, FL 33687

support@diverskillscenter.com

(813)802-4083

www.ingramcontent.com/pod-product-compliance
Lightning Source LLC
Chambersburg PA
CBHW061234180526
45170CB00003B/1299